DROPSHIPPING

Make Money Online: A Step By Step Guide On How To Start A Dropshipping Business – Amazon FBA, Ebay, Shopify

Marcus Baumann

this publication is strictly prohibited and any storage of this document is not allowed unless with written permission from the publisher. All rights reserved.

The information provided herein is stated to be truthful and consistent, in that any liability, in terms of inattention or otherwise, by any usage or abuse of any policies, processes, or directions contained within is the solitary and utter responsibility of the recipient reader. Under no circumstances will any legal responsibility or blame be held against the publisher for any reparation, damages, or monetary loss due to the information herein, either directly or indirectly.

Respective authors own all copyrights not held by the publisher.

The information herein is offered for informational purposes solely, and is universal as so. The presentation of the information is without contract or any type of guarantee assurance.

SOMMARIO

Dropship is aselling technique where the retailer does not stock goods. In the real world, the retailer provides a catalogue of goods to show to the customers. On the internet, an online store connects the customers and the wholesalers. However, in both cases, the dropshipper tries to sell the goods while acting as a liaison between the manufacturers or wholesalers and the customers. The profit of the dropshipper is the difference between the retail price and the wholesale price.

Dropshipping is popular nowadays because of the availability of the internet. Dropshipping is not essentially newly arrived; retailers are doing this in their brick and mortar stores for ages. However, in the past, they provided sample of the goods to be sold in their stores so that the customers have a chance of judging the quality of goods they want to purchase. Nowadays, it is pretty easy to have a website on the goods you want to sell. Modern dropshipping websites are known as online stores. The online stores provide in-depth review about the goods to be sold. They often build forums and FAQ sections to keep the customers well informed about the pros and cons of their products. The most popular dropship websites are designed in a way that the customers can know everything about their products by just visiting the websites.

Dropship businesses have the advantages of flexibilities and low capital cost. Virtually, you can dropship for free. You do not have to stock goods, so the initial cost is very low. Often the only cost is the cost to build a website for your business. You can start your business anytime and from anywhere in the world. You will just need a computer with internet connectivity.

Dropship businesses have certain drawbacks too. Internet is a crowded place, and there will be always much more competition in the cyber space than in the real world.

Lots of people are doing this now and the Search Engine Optimization (SEO) is now playing a very important role on making a website popular. You may find numerous online stores by conducting a single search for any product in any of the most popular search engines. Not all of these websites are genuine. In fact, often the top search results can be found as scams. However, these scams can genuinely affect your sales as these site builders are constantly doing SEO work to make their site come prior than yours.

There are certain things you have to keep in mind when conducting a dropship business. As you do not have your own stocks of goods, you have to keep yourself updated about the stock information of your wholesaler. If a customer orders a good from your online store, and after that you find out your wholesaler is out of stock, then the good will not arrive at time, and you are going to receive a bad review from the customer about your website.

If properly managed, dropshipping is a business that can offer you more financial security and personal freedom than any other business. USA dropship industry has provided livings for many people, and it is certainly possible for you to make money by dropshipping.

Dropshipping is a method of delivering products or items direct to your customer without you handling them. You act as the retailer, advertising the wares for sale with a mark up to cover your retailing type costs. You are effectively the seller (retailer) and accept payment direct from your customer for an order. The customer receives the product/s direct from the manufacturer without your customer knowing the point of source. Your profit in the transaction is the difference between the dropshippers price to you and retail price you have obtained for the items sold.

Dropshipping is advantageous to new and smaller retailers or shops because you do not need to hold or store stock and neither do you need to fund stock in advance of making a sale. Online sellers, individuals or businesses can take advantage of a dropshipping facility and advertise their inventory for sale as though the actual stock where their own.

The great thing about dropshipping is that you do not buy an item until you have already sold it. Not only do you benefit from having no inventory costs, you also profit from the difference between the wholesale and retail price. You will need to get the best price you can wholesale from your dropshipper or wholesaler in order to be as competitive as possible in the retail market.

The key to finding a dropshipper with the most room for profit for you is to get as close as possible to the manufacturer of any given product. If you find a niche market or the route to the manufacturer of a product or range of products you had like to sell' contact the manufacturer and ask if they already dropship or if they had consider doing so. Perhaps if they do not they can recommend one of their own distributors who does.

Once you have an arrangement with a recognised distributor, you can begin using their product information on your online outlets. Larger distributors may even have marketing assistance for you and smaller ones will let you download pictures and information from their own sites. Your distribution channel or dropshipper should always keep you up to date with new stock lines, stock levels and special offers or changing prices.

Dropshipping is an easy route to the online market and huge growth recently has highlighted and exacerbated potential problems that need to be avoided.

Dropship companies are all you need to expand your business online. This helps you to be a stockless retailer who does not have to make inventories about your items. A dropship company will help you ship all your items directly to your customers. Not having any troubles on inventories and room storage. Having the right dropship company for you would make your product line develop and would surely mean that customers will have better options. Better options for them and better sales for you.

Finding the right dropship company for your business is a must. They would not require any advance payments. It is surely convenient if you want doing your job in the comfort of your own home. First of all, drop shipping is done by selling the item and then getting the payment from the customer. The payment is then sent to your dropship supplier leaving behind your profit margin in your account. Make sure that you price the item competitively so you could gain enough profit. This kind of system makes your part easier with no initial investments made.

Your only primary concern is finding the right dropship company. Find the right one through signing up on any dropshipping websites you could find in the internet. A dropship directory can help you also. Make sure that in finding one, their lists of dropship companies are updated. If not, most probably you are entering in a scam.

To avoid these mistakes, a good dropship directory is when they would sell you lists of dropship suppliers. This guarantees you that they have spent the time researching, interviewing, and investigating the variety of dropshippers found in their list.

When you have chosen the right dropship company, make sure that you have read their terms regarding purchase of items you want to sell because some dropshipper's website would require a minimum purchase when you sign up. Then decide on an item you wish to sell. It is more profitable to sell items that are popular on eBay. Your dropshipper would provide you photos of your ordered items and descriptions as well. But the downside of this is that you will have many competitors who have the same

items and same descriptions. I suggest that you make your own creative description of it. It should be detailed and at the same time it can draw in buyers. Through this you can now confidently post your items and wait for customers to buy it.

The moment a buyer would like to buy your items. You have to contact your dropshipper through email or by filling up an online shipping form. Then you can pay your dropshipper using your credit card or any online payments. This is all you have to do when you have a dropship company by your side.

Your chosen dropship company should be reliable and would not let you down by shipping of the products and in providing customer support. Good variety of products should be offered and if possible brand new items. Once you have found the right dropship company you will grow long-standing relations with them. All you have to do is explore deeply e-commerce industries. With a little sacrifice, all will be worth it.

WHAT IS DROPSHIPPING?

Dropshipping is a supply chain management method in which the seller accepts payment for an order, but the customer receives the product directly from the manufacturer warehouse. In a dropshipping business model, the seller acts as a middleman between the manufacturer and the customer. His profit is the price difference between the wholesale and retail price of the item sold.

Can dropshipping really work? Yes and no. for some people it works very well, but for others it is a complete fail.

There Are Many Factors Involved In Making The Dropshipping Business Model Work, Such As:

1) *The Product Being Sold* - usually dropshipping works only with high quality products. If you try to sell a low quality product, then your customers will request a replacement or refund so you will be in big loss, since the shipping cost for the reverse logistics is going to be paid by you.

2) *The Price Of The Product* - if the product has a competitive price, than dropshipping business will work, but if your supplier will ask a higher price than your competitors, then the dropshipping business will not work for you.

3) *Delivery Time* - if your supplier can not ship the products fast, then your customers will be unsatisfied,probablyleaving you a bad reviews and sinking your reputation.

4) *Supplier Honesty* – A good supplier means very much. There have been many cases where suppliers cheated the sellers, sent defective or cheaply made products to the buyers, so it is very important with which supplier you start the dropshipping business

What Are The Benefits Of A Dropshipping Partnership?

Well, there are many benefits in a dropshipping partnership, but the most important ones are:

1) Lack Of Physical Inventory - since you sell using the dropshipping business method, all the products will be stored at your supplier warehouse, saving you lots of money on maintaining stock in a warehouse.

2) Increased Products In Your Online Store - since you do not store the products you sell, you are not limited by your warehouse size in selling as many products as you want, on your online store. You may even sell products from multiple suppliers in your online store.

3) *Reduces Shipping Prices* - usually the manufacturers that do dropshipping get lower prices on shipping prices due to the fact that they ship thousands of products every day and they get better shipping quotes from the shipping companies.

So far so good. It looks like dropshipping is the right thing to do when selling online. But just as with anything that has a positive side, dropshipping also has a negative side. So what are the risks and hidden costs involved in a dropshipping partnership?

First of all, the main risk involved in a dropshipping business is that your supplier may scam you. He may send you a different product or even a defective product, and later to claim that the product broke during transportation. And the cost of sending the product back would be covered by you, the seller. Another major risk comes from the buyers. Buyers can scam too. They may receive the product, and later claim that the transaction was not authorized by them, and that someone used their credit

card without permission, so they would file a chargeback on you leaving you with no money and no product. Another downside of dropshipping is that the wholesale price of the dropshipped products is higher than buying them in bulk, so this is a point also worth focusing at.

DROPSHIPPING - STARTING SUCCESSFULLY!

The whole spectrum of doing business has undergone a world of change in the last few decades. One of the latest online business ideas is dropship services. This online business involves a process in which manufacturers or suppliers deliver the products directly to the customers of the dropship business without the business having to pre-purchase or stock the goods. The best part of the bargain is that the business owner, or reseller, does not have to do any hard work such as inventing, designing,

buying or making the product, testing the market, describing the product on the website, making the website attractive, or promoting the product.

The dropship services business owner just has to list the products on eBay and get orders for the products by using its own or the supplying company's descriptions and graphics. When the orders are received, the reseller supplies the information regarding the buyers' names and addresses and other details of the order, so that the supplier can send the products to the buyer. The company also collects the payment.

The business of dropship services can reap rich returns for the business owner, but the most important dropshipping guide is that it is necessary to take care of the business and customers to ensure that any buyers' complaints regarding poor product quality or delays between receipt of payments and delivery of goods are tended to promptly. Any negligence in providing necessary after-sales services and attending to complaints can tarnish the image of the company and lead to loss of revenue and future orders. In order to find an answer to how to dropship and how to start a dropshipping business, it is vital to select a reliable supplier. The wrong selection can have disastrous results.

Follow The Following Steps Before Starting This Type Of Business.

1) Select Recommended Suppliers: The first step for starting a dropship services business is that the sourcing of the suppliers should be done with great care. Simply select the suppliers recommended by other people. It is possible to get free or paid-for lists of dropshipping companies on Internet directory sites. Some give accurate information whereas others might be owned by unscrupulous suppliers, so avoid those particular recommendations.

2) Check The Contact Details: Once a selection is made based on reliable recommendations, and after checking that the range of products that the business intends to deal are sold by the supplier, check the contact details provided by the supplier. Pertinent contact information such as phone number, email address, and a mailing address should be available on the supplier's website. Avoid any supplier with incorrect or with no contact information at all. Make sure the phone is answered and see how long it takes for the supplier to answer emails, which may come in handy later if you have a reason to contact them with a problem.

3) Check Business Terms: Since there can be disputes with the supplier regarding faulty goods or undelivered items, business terms and conditions of the supplier should be properly stated and understood by the reseller. Realize that the responsibilities of the business as a reseller are different than the responsibilities that the supplier would have toward the reseller.

4) Unreasonable Subscription Fees: As a reseller, the dropship services business has to pay resellers registration fees and, in some cases, ongoing subscription charges for the right to access the supplier's catalogue. Access for a limited time is normally allowed before registration. Before registering with any supplier, check whether it charges ongoing subscription fees. Fine print should also be checked well for any between-the-lines clauses.

5) Beware of Middlemen Disguised as Suppliers: Check whether the potential supplier holds enough stock of the products and they are not a middleman posing as a supplier. These middlemen place orders with the real supplier and when they receive orders from the reseller and, in this process, long delays can take place. These delays can result in losses to the customer and subsequent losses to the reseller because the payment would have to be refunded.

6) *Modes of Payment:* Find out how the supplier expects to receive payments because the most convenient mode would be the same by which the customer pays the reseller.This will save charges and time. It is also advisable to avoid having to pay by Wire Transfer or Telegraph Transfer because the risk is higher if there is no customer protection.

7) *Beware of Companies Selling Fake Goods:* While choosing a supplier, avoid those sites that offer branded goods such as designer clothing and electrical goods at unbelievably low prices. Such low priced, so-called designer goods are bound to be fake unless the supplier is trustworthy and renowned and he has obtained the goods from a close-out, or if the goods are refurbished or Grade A returns. If the reseller sells fake goods, he can be accused of selling counterfeit goods.

8) Look for Web Reviews: Having short-listed a few suppliers, it would be helpful to seek out reviews and comments regarding the companies on Internet forums from other dropship resellers. Although it might be difficult to find any good comments since the resellers would not like others to know about their profitable source, bad reviews can certainly help in making the right decision.

9) Look for Artists and Craftsmen: Teaming up with artists and craftsmen for their creative products is a unique way to do dropship services business. These creative people usually lack marketing savvy. Visits to local craft fairs can provide unlimited opportunities to get stunning creative items at unbelievably low prices as compared to eBay prices. The dropship business need not buy these items, but an arrangement could be worked out for working on commission. They will likely be happy to take his payment and deliver the products to the buyer of the dropship business when a sale is made.

Dropshipping is an excellent option to start an online retail venture with little investment. The products you choose to dropship is critical to the profitability of you business. So, before you plan to do dropshipping online decide on the products you are planning to dropship. The next step would involve identifying the reliable supplier's who can dropship the product to your consumers. Choosing a supplier for your product is a trial and error process. The best option I would suggest would be to buy a sample product from them and analyse the quality of the product. If you are satisfied with their product, then stick to the supplier if the profit margin you could achieve is satisfactory. This is basic step to identify quality supplier for your product. If you are focussing on huge number of products,

27

identifying a reliable supplier for each of those products can become a tedious and time consuming process.

Here is when Dropship Services come into play. The role of a Dropship Service is to do all the dealings with the supplier and hence reducing your effort in identifying quality suppliers. Most of the dropship services validate the authenticity of the supplier making sure you get the products on time if ordered. There are quite a few Dropship Services available namely *Doba, Worldwidebrands, Dropship Access, SaleHoo etc...*

Before deciding on the Dropship option that is suitable for you, list down the following:

- Product(s) you are planning to dropship
- Amount you could invest
- Do you prefer to try the service before subscribing?
- Are you planning to sell the products on eBay?

Most of the dropship services charge you a monthly fee or upfront one-off payment in order to use their services. If you are new to dropshipping, you can try dropship service like Doba which offers a free 7-day trial. This would be a sufficient time to figure out whether dropship service is suitable for you. Your decision should be based on the availability of the product you are planning to dropship and the suppliers you have access to. Another advantage is **Doba** is eBay certified meaning you can dropship products available through Doba on eBay.

SaleHoo is another great dropship service if you are new to dropshipping. Not only they guarantee you a supplier they also offer a 60-day money back guarantee if you are not satisfied. This would be a reasonable time to figure out whether your business model can work for you. If you have some experience in dropshipping then I would highly recommend **Worldwidebrands**. They are also a lot cheaper when compared to Doba and SaleHoo as they only charge you a one-off fee. The suppliers available are verified to meet the business standards. If you are already into dropshipping and would like a reliable dropshipping service then Worldwidebrands is definitely a service to checkout.

STREAMLINE YOUR ONLINE BUSINESS PROCESSES WITH THE POWER OF DROPSHIP PRODUCTS

Why Does the Dropship Product Business Model Succeed?

The key advantage of choosing a dropship product business model for your existing or prospective online storefront is that the dropship company will stock, store and ship out the products for you, thereby saving you precious time and energy.

In other words, every time that a product is sold through your website, the dropship company will take care of extracting the needed item, packing it up for shipment, and then sending it on to the client who ordered it.

By utilizing this clever method of streamlining your online business, you will be able to focus on other aspects of running your day-to-day operation, while leaving the packing and shipping to the dropship company.

Do Dropship Services Have Disadvantages?

Of course, dropship services are this type are not free. Therefore, it is vital to comparison-shop for the most affordable and reliable dropship services. However, when you work with a reputable company, you will find that dropship services are actually extremely cost-effective. Because paying for dropship services is really the only "con" involved with the entire process, getting a great deal on your preferred services will ensure that you enjoy practical business support, without any drawbacks.

Since time is money, outsourcing the task of packing and shipping items to your chosen dropship company may actually be a great way to save cash in the long run.

That is why today's smartest, savviest entrepreneurs are choosing to work with stellar dropship companies that offer affordable rates, as well as products which fit their niches to perfection.

Find a Dropship Service that Fits Your Online Niche

In addition to finding an affordable dropship company, you must ensure that your preferred dropship service offers the sort of merchandise that you really want to sell. For example, if you are interested in selling the most impressive brands to your online clientele, you will need to find a dropship supplier that is able to offer premier brands which have the instant "name recognition" that your customers will look for. Conversely, if you want to sell generic products which offer supreme value to your online clientele, you must seek out a dropshipper which is able to offer this type of inventory.

The basic business model is not complicated. When you sign on with a dropshipper, you will be able to advertise their products through your website. The dropship supplier will give you images that you may use in order to promote your online inventory. Then, when a customer buys what you are offering, the dropship company will spring into action, by packing and shipping out the item.

Dropshipping is an easy and uncomplicated way to streamline any type of online enterprise. If you want to sell products online, but you just do not have the space to store an inventory (or the time and energy to ship products out yourself), you will find that dropship services make it so easy to get your business up and running.

Before selecting the right dropship service for you, do a little shopping around. Once you have found a reputable company, which offers the right products for the most affordable prices, you will be ready to make the task of running an online business so much easier.

FINDING DROPSHIPPING WHOLESALERS YOURSELF

The Problem

As dropshipping becomes more and more prevalent in online retailing, it would seem that dropshipping wholesalers would announce themselves and their programs directly to consumers through search engine marketing and other online visibility efforts. In reality, however, network effects and other factors prevent new dropship business owners from readily finding quality dropshipping wholesalers through efforts of their own.

First, there is the problem of dropshipping scams. You have likely heard plenty about this trend, so there is little use in beating a dead horse any further. The fact of the matter is that dropshipping scams do exist and will likely exist as long as there are unsuspecting dropship business owners out there to prey on.

Second, there is the aforementioned network effects. Dropshipping wholesalers want to concentrate their promotional efforts (insofar as they relate to the promotion of their dropshipping programs) to those online communities where they will find the most qualified dropshippers. These communities exist in directory programs such as **Worldwide Brands, Salehoo and others.** Just as dropshippers try to avoid scams, so too do wholesalers. There is an additional level of pre-qualification that goes along with membership in these directories that benefits both wholesalers and dropshippers.

The Benefit of Dropshipping Wholesale Directory Programs

Many of these directory programs cost money, so it is necessary to weigh the benefits with the costs of such investments. There are a number of benefits to dropshippers of membership in such programs.

First of all, dropshippers save a great deal of time and money in avoiding dropshipping scams (for the most part). Dropshipping wholesalers who attain membership in these programs have been screened for a variety of factors aimed to determine the legitimacy of their droppshipping programs. This saves dropshippers time and money.

Members of these programs also benefit from the economies of scale afforded to dropship member programs. A sole proprietor has little bargaining power against a large manufacturer, wholesaler or distributor in negotiating for the terms of (or even consideration for) a dropshipping agreement.

Finally, many offer additional resources, useful partnerships and other value-adds that assist new dropshippers in the launch of their business. Worldwide Brands offers a free license of Quickbooks and a wealth of extremely helpful tools aimed at helping get dropshippers started on the right foot.

The bottom line is that there are a number of benefits to investing in access to quality Dropshipping Wholesalers. Consider the costs and the benefits in making your decision. If you have extra time and money to spend during the initial stages of dropship business development, you may not need or want to pay for such a directory service. If, on the other hand, you want to make a solid investment that will serve you well throughout the lifetime of your business, consider a smart investment in a dropship membership program.

A wholesale dropship is a great way to make money online. This form of ecommerce removes many of the stresses of selling items online and has become a great way to start a trade business, so find out how to make money by wholesale dropshipping.

During the last decade the internet has reached the homes of most people around the planet, and it has revolutionized the way we buy and sell products. During that time people have been looking for ways to make money from internet trading, and one of the most promising ways is to enter into wholesale dropshipping. By using a wholesale dropship you can buy and sell items and make money online, but how?

Firstly it is important to understand what a wholesale dropship is. Dropshipping is a new and exciting way to conduct ecommerce and works by a dropship company buying goods directly from the manufacturer, at pre-sale rates, which it then stores. Clients of the dropship company can then sell the goods they have in stock and make the after sale profit, before giving a percentage to the dropship company of course.

- *Save On Shipping*

Perhaps the major advantage of using a dropship company is the fact that they handle the goods, and they distribute the goods. As the seller you do not have to worry about seeing the products and more importantly shipping them, it is a business model that allows you to profit but never have the worry of whether the goods make it to their destination, because the expert dropshipping company will do that for you.

Basically the dropshipping company becomes your personal stock holder and distributer, and it is possible to build a strong working relationship together. If this does indeed happen you can get your distributer to place your company logo onto boxes, which further advertises your brand and products.

- ***Get More Customers***

If you are an online seller then you will likely have a website that advertises your goods, and using the wholesale dropship model you will be a fully-fledged

ecommerce store. Search engines love a quality ecommerce store, and you could well rank highly on Google search which ultimately will bring more customers, more sales, and more revenue.

- ***Easy To Do***

Everything about the wholesale dropship business is easy, from not handling goods, to not dealing with distribution. Also it is very easy to find a droppshipping company, in fact there are hundreds of them available, and all offer you the chance to distribute goods worldwide for profit without ever having to deal with the stresses of normal business practises.

Think of wholesale dropshipping as a different kind of selling, you are like the checkout assistant, you just deal with the money and the customers while other take care of the stress, but the big difference is that you will be reaping a great reward. This is still a relatively new way to make money online so there is still plenty of money to be made in a growing market that is still open for new businesses.

DROPSHIP MANUFACTURERS – KEY FACTOR TO WHOLESALE DROPSHIPPING!

Are you looking into starting your own wholesale dropship business but are weary of the initial cash injection to buy inventory? Well do not be. With dropship manufacturers you can easily source designer products at heavily reduced prices and best of all, you do not ned to hand over money until your customer pays you.

Locating dropship manufacturers has become an easy task in this day and age. However, finding a reliable dropship manufacturer is a different story. Inevitably, tracing brand name items at low cost is an art of dealing closely with the dropship manufacturer. A wholesale dropship business in this day and age requires little time investment once you find the supplier and the product you wish to sell.

Having reliable dropship manufacturers alleviates any stress that your product will not reach the customer. Once you have established your wholesale dropship business start negotiating with the dropshipping company on prices. You will be surprised how easily you can get better prices just by meeting certain targets each month.

There is no better time to start a dropship business and look for dropship manufacturers. With the recession gradually fading out and more jobs becoming available in the future, you will be nicely placed to dominate the niche you choose to get involved in.

Dropship manufacturers are the key in succeeding and making money online. Everyday people come to the internet to find a new way of making money or getting out of a dead end job and dropshipping is by far the most popular. It is not by accident that this is the most popular, drop shipping is making people full time incomes from their homes and it could help you succeed also.

If you are familiar with this business model, you are aware that finding dropship manufacturers is paramount to take your wholesale dropship business to a totally new level. The best thing about this type of business is that you can start selling on eBay, the largest online auction marketplace, without having a website. You also do not even need to store inventory. The dropship manufacturers do this on your behalf. There are 100s of products online that you could look at selling in your drop ship business.

A website is not necessary to get starting to become an online dropshipper. However, if you are selling consistently you should start to think about building a website and bring your eBay dropship business to a new level. Do not leave all those customers untapped.

My advice is to start one niche dropship business and if that is successful diverge into other niches. Then look for other dropship manufacturers. Increase your portfolio of niches and believe me you will be successful selling online.

REAL WHOLESALE DROPSHIP COMPANIES

When you are starting in the wholesale dropship business. The company that provides the products you sell can make or break your business before you even start. With the marketplace flooded with middlemen, finding a real wholesale dropship company is hardly an easy task.

Real wholesale dropship companies are harder to find because no one wants to share their secret little niche wholesaler with everyone, they think by doing this,they will lose their bread and butter. While this may hold some validity, we that buy wholesale directory have a different take on the situation. We believe that wholesale dropship sources should be available to all, at no cost. With the internet as vast as it is, finding these wholesale dropship companies can be a pain, but with time and research, you should be able to find a wholesale dropship company that can make your business grow and be profitable for you.

The trick to finding real wholesale dropship companies is to know the warning signs of the middlemen. These middlemen have one common denominator, and that is to take your money while you do most of the work. Below are some tips to look for when choosing a wholesale dropship company.

Is there any fee? If a wholesale dropship company charges a fee for membership, this may be a sign that it is not a real wholesale dropship company. Some real wholesale dropshippers do charge a fee for membership, but it is usually to cover credit apps, processing, etc. which will not be a recurring fee.

Phone number and address available? A true wholesale dropship company will list phone numbers and their physical address. If they have a warehouse that contains 60,000 products, odds are there is an address for that warehouse.

Is their products rehashed images from some other website, or are they original. When a company has physical possession of a product, odds are that the image they use is their own, and not copied from some other location. Middlemen may use images of products copied from somewhere else on the web, simply because they do not have possession of the product they intend to sell to you.They are using dropshipping also, which will cut into your profits.

While there are other warning signs to look for when choosing a real wholesale drophip company its best to remember these tips when choosing a wholesale dropshipper.

Other tips for wholesale dropship companies include making sure you have a tax id. True wholesale dropshippers will need your tax id to do business with you if they are a true wholesaler. Not having a tax id will definitely make your hunt for a real wholesale dropship company harder. Tax ids are not costly and only require a bit of time to complete the necessary forms and reports. In short, get a tax id, and find true wholesale dropship companies to support your new business.

BUILDING YOUR DROPSHIPPING BUSINESS ON THESE MAJOR ELEMENTS

Dropshipping is a process of selling products without having to stock or store any items. Dropshipping is very easy way to get started online especially for the first timer looking to take that leap and start their own business.

Dropshipping is a very popular method of selling products online. Believe it or not dropshipping is a good business if you do it right.

In the some part of the world, dropshipping is a massive business. Dropshipping is a very popular phenomena in those places and is very quickly spreading in other regions of the world. The starting place for the majority of dropshippers is the eBay auction site.This is how they advertise the products for the companies and the companies do the shipping.Dropshipping is a wonderful way to start a home based or small wholesale business. Actually, dropshipping is based on exactly the idea that you do not have enough money to start a traditional, full-sized company. It is great for the companies that wish to keep their branding and very profitable for their partners that promote their products.

The way they do dropshipping is they charge you their wholesale prices (50% off most items) and then they ship directly to your customer. Dropshipping is the biggest boom business going and sales are now hitting multi billions a year.

The convenience of using dropshipping is there is no middle man, your order comes direct from the company. One of the biggest benefits of dropshipping is that you do not ever have to handle the merchandise.

Dropshipping is a unique marketing method that allows you to sell by mail or online without carrying one single book in your inventory. Just like in any business, there are risks involved when it comes to dropshipping. However to really generate any money, you had better strive to search for your products at a sale cost.

Whether you promote products on eBay, Amazon Stores or your own website, The easiest way to make money with these products is to learn to sell on eBay. Dropshipping is a great way to start an eBay or online business IF you do your homework, take your time, and investigate all the options available to you.

If you are looking to develop your own eBay selling business without investment in stock, dropshipping is the way for you.

The Elements

1) Make sure the dropshipping company does not have any complaints against them.

2) Ask the dropshipping company if they supply tracking numbers for the products and the time it takes for them to ship the item.

3) Let your customers know that they will be receiving the item from the supplier and that they dropship for you.

4) Communicate with your customers anytime a problem may occur.

5) Do business with more than 1 dropshipper.

6) Consider ordering a few test products from the dropshipper before you begin business, to be sure of their reliability and accuracy in filling orders.

7) You should be able to get the products at a low price and sell the products for a profit.

8) Start with low orders to get comfortable with the dropshipping company and then build up to large orders.

You could be in business and taking your first orders by this time tomorrow. Anyone can start their own home business buying and selling goods. Start a home based business dropshipping on eBay or your own ecommerce website. If you are short on money and would like to start a profitable business, I would consider dropshipping the ideal place to start.

SIGNIFICANCE OF A DROPSHIP FORUM

A dropship forum is a great place for merchants to network with other retailers and look for solutions and ideas for establishing, running and expanding their dropshipping businesses. The economic crisis, which began in some years back, has forced many retailers to shun conventional methods of doing business and move to the dropshipping business model. Dropshipping allows online retailers to sell their products without the need of buying supplies and hiring manpower to take care of packaging and shipping. As a result, this business model has become quite popular.

Having said that, dropshipping has its own problems. The most common one is getting a good dropshipper on whom you can rely for quality products and good customer service. As a result, many dropship forums have come into being so that online retailers can come together, share their views and experiences, and overcome the problems posed by dropshippers.

The Key Benefits Of A Dropship Forum:

• Get References

Often, the retailers who are new to the dropship business do not know who to contact for dropshipping services. These retailers could get references from a dropship directory or a dropship forum.

- ***Get Feedback***

Getting references alone is not sufficient. Before dealing with a dropshipper, you should get feedback about them from retailers who have used their services. There have been a number of dropshipping scams, and therefore, getting feedback is absolutely essential to know more about a dropshipper and what to expect while dealing with them.

- ***Get Expert Opinions***

A dropship forum usually has several experienced and successful retailers that can help you solve your problems. For example, if you are facing dropshipping problems, like late delivery of items, items out of stock, or no response from customer service, you could get expert opinions on how to sort out these issues. Dropship forums help you get mentors that can help you make your business successful.

- ***Get Honest Opinions***

The ideas and opinions expressed in forums are usually genuine. Unlike newspapers and magazines where reporters and writers have their vested interests, forums consists of retailers that express their true opinions and experiences. However, the instance of a dropshipper posing as a retailer to advertise and promote their services cannot be ruled out.

- ***Networking***

Dropship forums allow you to expand your business network. Networking is important to get business and the latest updates and news of the business world. All this helps you in long run.

Though there are many advantages of a dropship forum, you have to be careful while forming networks and following the advice of retailers on a forum. They could have a vested interest, and therefore, you should guard yourself. However, if you work and act smartly, you could benefit a lot from dropship forums.

• *It Helps You To Get Product Ideas*

The business environment is constantly changing. You cannot sell the same products all the time. The products that are in demand today may become outdated tomorrow.

Therefore, you need to keep a close eye on the market to know about product trends. In case you find doing the research on product ideas difficult, a dropship forum could help you. These forums keep updated and useful information on how to choose your products, which products are the most profitable and which products you should avoid. Though there are many advantages of a dropshipping forum, you should ensure that you choose the right one. Some dropship firms run forums in order to promote their services. They may not give you honest opinions about different dropship services. Therefore, before heeding anybody's advice, you should do your own research as well.

SOME CONSIDERED OR SUGGESTED SITES FOR DROPSHIPPING BUSINESS

To dropship or not to dropship, that is the question. If you are thinking of using a wholesale dropship supplier as part of your supply chain management technique and you look one way then you see glowing reviews of the system with people saying their customers are happier, they are making more money and it cleans 90% of all difficult carpet stains.

But if you turn the other way you hear horror stories about how a particular eBay trader's seller reputation went down the toilet simply because they had chosen to chance their arm with a particular dropship company.

So what is the real story? Is dropshipping a blessing or a curse and who should you believe?

Much like cooking the secret of dropshipping successfully, whether it is electronics you are dropshipping or clothes, is in where and how you get the source and how much work you put into the preparation.

In fact doing background research into potential wholesale dropship firms is often the difference between a successful partnership and a sunk business.

Here are some websites and internet services that will not only save you money when tracking down a wholesale dropship supplier but cost absolutely nothing to use:

1) Whois : While the internet may seem like a big world of anonymous entities there are several whois services online that will let you know which website belongs to who, the best-known of which is probably Whois.net. Simply by entering the URL of the wholesale dropship service into the search bar you will be able to see who owns the site, how long they have owned it and if they own any other sites. If you want to do any more detailed analysis a paid report will give you more information but you should get most of what you need from the free search.

2) Reseller rating : Resellerrating.com is a website where you can check out user reviews of sites and see what vendors like you think of products and how well they sell.

3) Dropship Forum : A UK based e-commerce forum, dropshipforum.co.uk, has a fantastic section, dropship watch where you can check out to see if anybody else has had any unpleasant experience with a particular China dropshipping company or wholesale dropship company.Another forum which casts its net a little wider is:

4) The Wholesale Forums : Thewholesaleforums.co.uk will help you out with more than peer reviews on wholesale dropship sources, there is a whole raft of useful information on the site.

5) Rateitall.com : The destination if you want to see what anybody thinks of anything. Rateitall has reviews on everything from China dropship companies, electronic appliances, phone companies, movies and many many more topics.

HOW TO GET A RELIABLE DROPSHIPPING REVIEW

Reading this book will probably means that you are in the hunt for a good dropship firm and a reliable dropshipping review source. Though there are many websites that provide reviews on wholesalers and dropshippers, you should not trust them blindly, as the reviewers could have vested interests. So, the question is, where can you find reliable dropshipping reviews?

1. Get Opinions From Your Acquaintances

You must have some friends and acquaintances in the retailing or wholesaling business. You should consult them before signing up with a dropshipping firm in order to get reviews and feedback about the firm. It might be that some of them have used its services. Some may not have used its services but may have heard about it.

Therefore, family, friends, and colleagues could be reliable dropshipping review sources. They could give you honest and unbiased opinions.

2. Visit Dropship Forums

Retailers are increasingly using dropship forums to get references and reviews on dropshippers. Apart from enabling them to hire the right dropshippers, dropship forums also help retailers in expanding their business networks and getting solutions to their dropshipping problems. You could become a member of a dropship forum to get reviews and opinions on a given dropshipping service. If you are not interested in becoming a member, you could just check the review threads as a visitor at their websites.

IS DROPSHIPPING STILL THE BUSINESS OPPORTUNITY IT USED TO BE?

You could ask the dropshipping firm to give references of their clients.This would enable you to speak to their clients and get their opinions. If the dropshipping firm is not keen on sharing this information, then it is likely that they do not provide good service and therefore do not like their prospective clients to interact with their past and present clients.

Getting a reliable dropshipping review source is difficult but not impossible. There are some wholesale review that provide true and extensive information about dropshippers, which is required by retailers in hiring decisions. These websites ensure that they collect information from several reliable sources rather than from middlemen and scammers. Apart from reviewing the services of dropshippers, they also review their products.

Dropshipping Used To Be So Easy

Going back a couple of years, most people looking to set up a dropship business would choose, what was at the time, the simplest business model for success. You would see what products were selling, find a supplier for your drop ship products, and then simply list them on one of the biggest marketplaces in the world, eBay, and wait for them to sell. With the millions of people who were looking to buy items on eBay everyday, as long as you had the dropship products they wanted to buy, at the right price, it was one of the easiest and fastest ways to start making money with dropshipping.

eBay Is No Longer The Key Ingredient For Dropship Success

Fast forward a few years and for most dropshipping businesses, eBay no longer provides the opportunity it once did. As the world's biggest online auction site has grown, there are more and more sellers offering the same items, and customers who are only interested in buying at increasingly lower prices. For dropship businesses who have to add their eBay fees onto the cost of sourcing and shipping their drop ship products to the customer, profit margins have got smaller and smaller, until it no longer makes sense to use eBay if they want to make a profit. Click, if you want to know more about drop shipping.

What Has Changed, And What Does This Mean For The Future?

So is this the end for dropship opportunities? Hardly. What is does mean is that those who have the right approach, and see it as a business rather than some kind of get rich quick scheme, have adapted to maintain the kind of profits that will sustain their dropshipping business. They now look at other ways of marketing their dropship products; Amazon, their own websites, Search Engine Optimization and Social Media.

Has it become more challenging to develop a profitable dropship business? Possibly. But running any business is a challenge, which is why it is worth it when you get it right. If anything, the changes in the dropshipping market will mean that it becomes less attractive for those looking for a quick buck, and who generally give the industry a bad name. Which means that the professional dropship businesses will continue to grow - great for them, and for the customers. Also, more and more people will start to see dropshipping as a way to get started, before developing their enterprise using other business models. With its low cost of entry and sustainability, dropshipping is a way for ecommerce businesses to establish themselves, so they can gain the investment capital and experience needed to move on and start using traditional wholesale suppliers, who offer greater profit potential.

While the concept of dropshipping has not really changed, how you need to approach it in order to be successful certainly has.Those who still see selling dropship products as an easy way to make some quick money, will not doubt end up being the ones that say a dropship business can not succeed. While those who approach it as they would any other new business startup, investing time and effort, and looking to grow their business with a view to the long term, will be the ones that prove a dropship business can still be a great opportunity.

SOME DISCOURAGING FACTORS ABOUT DROPSHIP BUSINESS-PLEASE NOTE!

Dropshipping is getting a lot of good reviews from people and sellers who are successful in this kind of business, but surely there are pitfalls in dropshipping that most sellers do not share;

especially if they themselves are selling dropship directories and the like.

Here are the factors;

- ***Trial and Error* –**

Scouting for a reliable dropshipping company can be a very difficult task. These companies will always have their best foot forward when you are talking terms with them but it is a different story when you are already selling their products and you encounter a problem. It becomes a cat and mouse thing or even maybe a hide and seek process. Very frustrating.

- ***Quality issues* –**

One of the best things about a dropship business is also the worst thing about it. Since you do not stock inventory, there is no way for you to check on the quality of the products being sent to your customers. Not until you get a phone call or an email from an irate customer. And defending yourself is a little difficult since you probably haven't seen the product yourself, physical, I mean.

- ***Attracting customers –***

Some customers shy away from dropshippers. This is either because they have had bad experience in the past or they think that they are paying more than what they should, which is true because you have to add to the price so you can make money. This is the reason why people who owns a dropshipbusiness normally would not say that their products are drop ship.

- ***Unpredictable –***

Since you do not own the business you are at the mercy of the dropshipping company's existence. Not unless you happened to partner with the most stable and the most reliable business around, you could be out of business tomorrow.

So those are my four reasons why a dropship business may not be good. But of course since there are a lot of successful dropshippers, it only shows that there is a way around all these, and like what I always say, research and preparation is the key to successful dropship business.

AVOID DROPSHIPPING TRICKS

Although dropshipping is not a new business concept, it is a method of order fulfillment that your average retail customer is totally oblivious to. Many online sellers who only actively sell on auction sites such as eBay often stumble across the term 'dropship' and only then realise the merits and potential of reselling on this basis. For many, the realisation of the vast range of goods available to resell on a dropship basis is instrumental in their progression from selling unwanted household items and clothing to smartening up their image and advertising shiny new factory sealed branded goods, with many opening online retail stores instead, or as well as advertising in their usual way.

For many who progress along this route, the reselling activity with their dropship supplier will be a long lasting, fruitful and profitable one, without any major issues arising to sour their business relationship but for many others the whole experience of starting out using a dropship supplier will be an absolute nightmare one that could ruin their online business, their reputation and cost them a fortune financially.

The horror stories are plentiful, with so many companies now advertising top range branded goods at unbelievably low prices for dropshipping resellers, if you hook up with the wrong one, you may find that once they have taken your orders and your money they then fail to deliver the goods, or commonly what they do send is not a the real mccoy which means that you are left to appease your irate buyer, refunding their purchase money along with their postage costs. This then means you are the one who is out of pocket along with that dreaded tarnished reputation. Think about it, if you have made a handful of orders with your new supplier and each one is not fulfilled, in a short space of time you will need to refund your buyers and that could be a lot of cash.

There is a very simple checklist that anyone new to dropshipping should use to verify their suppliers. Its not bulletproof but by following a few simple steps, the risk of costly disasters can be reduced.

1. Sourcing Dropship Suppliers -The best dropshippers to use are the ones that are recommended, there are many advertising on the web and they all promise the best deals but its the benefit of other peoples experiences that gets you the right one. There are many 'directory sites' listed on the internet offering free or paid for lists of dropshipping companies, some may be good and offer accurate information but then there are many that are owned and compiled by the suppliers themselves listing only their companies details, so best to avoid to be safe.

2. *Contact Details* -Once you have found a supplier that sells the range of items that you are looking to stock, check out the contact details on their site. Any legitimate business encourages contact with customers, after all that is how to get more business done. The suppliers site should clearly display a contact phone number, physical location address and e-mail details. If they do, try them out, see if the phone gets answered, test the response time to your e-mail because in future if you encounter problems with any orders you may place, you need assurance they are on hand to deal with them. Avoid any supplier site with incorrect or no contact information.

3. *Terms and Conditions* -All dropship suppliers should clearly state their terms of business and it is strongly advisable to familiarise yourself with them. You need to know where you stand when issues arise such as undelivered items or faulty goods received, if you have doubts or questions then e-mail a request for clarification.Remember, this falls into Business to Business contract legislation and in most countries it will vary greatly from the laws that cover Business to Public, in other words, as a reseller you will have different responsibilities to your customer than your supplier has to you.

4. Registration and Subscription Fees -It is common practice for dropshipping companies to charge their resellers registration fees and possibly ongoing subscription charges to access their catalogue and it is widely acceptable. In most cases, if you contact these suppliers before registering they will normally allow you access to the prices for a limited time or maybe e-mail you a sample price list. Always tread carefully with any site that charges ongoing subscription fees, dip your toe in the water first with the shortest time possible and double check the paperwork to ensure that you do not inadvertently sign up for any lengthy minimum period that will incur costs for unwanted membership.

5. Stock Levels and Dispatch Times -When communicating with any potential dropship company, always enquire about the amount of stock they carry. A lot of suppliers will show stock levels on their sites but many advertise themselves as wholesale or dropshippers when in fact they are purely middlemen or agents and only place orders with their supplier when enough orders are placed by resellers that meet minimum order quantity restrictions they have. If you end up with a middleman it could mean lengthy and unacceptable delays for your customers to receive their goods, which potentially means you having to refund.

6. *Accepted Payment Methods-* There are numerous online payment methods available and all of them incur costs that need to factored into the selling prices, PayPal, Nochex, Google Checkout to name a few. When choosing your dropshipping supplier always confirm how they expect to receive payment, ideally you want them to accept payments the same way that you do from your customers as that is where the funds will be held and you will save time and charges if this is the case. Many overseas suppliers will expect payment by Wire Transfer or Telegraphi Transfer and this is high risk without any customer protection that you have with the processors like PayPal. Initially, it is advisable to steer clear from this method unless you have built a solid and trusting relationship with your supplier.

7. *Branded Goods-* One quick internet search will find countless sites offering designer clothing and the latest top brand electrical goods at a fraction of their retail price available for dropship. In short - Steer Clear. Unless you are ordering the goods from a known and trusted supplier that has sourced some close out, refurbished or Grade A returns you can almost guarantee that branded or designer goods that are priced too good to be true will be fake and reselling these could mean that you as the retailer face the consequences of dealing in counterfiet goods.

8. *Web Search Reviews* -Once you have found a potential dropship supplier or compiled a shortlist, then take the time to do a quick internet search of the company names. It should throw up some interesting listings and normally amongst them will be reviews or comments made in Forums or Blog pages from prior or existing fellow dropship resellers. The chances are that you will find more bad comments than good as any happy resellers are less likely to post about their fantastic dropshipping supplier and tip off the whole world of their money making arrangement but the bad posts should speak for themselves and will assist you in your judgement.

By following this simple checklist you are not guaranteed overnight riches and success when dropship selling as it just covers some of the fundamental basics for anyone starting out. The hope is, that it portrays the need for diligence when in business and will avert some from making costly mistakes by jumping in feet first with the first dropship company that they find.

There are many dropshipping companies that can be very helpful in extending your business.

In fact, these companies have become very common due to the pivotal role they played in increasing the profit of different business companies.

As the number of dropshipping companies is increasing and so is the number of scammers. So it has become very difficult to find a good dropshipping company. If you are also in search of a good dropshipping company, then do not worry because all your worries are about to disappear after reading this book.

The first thing that you must consider before hiring any dropshipping company is its **repute.** Only reputable and trustworthy dropshipper companies can serve in your purpose. Many people resort to eBay to look for getting supplier lists. This is not the right way because those lists are either outdated or those companies are no more in dropshipping business.

The best option for finding dropshipping ventures is to check online. You will find a variety of good and affordable wholesale and dropship sites on the internet. But at the same time, there are many scammers who can ensnare you on internet. So it is always better to ask for a sample product from your desirable dropshipping companies. There are also some directories of dropshipping companies on internet. Always check those directories, compiled by reputable companies, to get more information about various dropshipping companies present on the scene at present.

The good dropshipping companies are those who address the complaints of their customers instantaneously. In other words, they have also a good customer care service.

So it is always recommended that you choose that dropshipping company for your business who has addressed maximum number of complaints of their customers.

If you are able to find a good dropshipping company, then you will see that the sales of your products would increase reasonably and you will earn more profit. The useful role of dropship companies in extending your business is proven and you must not have any doubt regarding it.

WHAT YOU NEED TO KNOW BEFORE YOU DROPSHIP ITEMS

You have decided to dropship items. You have seen other people making good money being a dropshipper and you want to have your slice of the pie.

One of the main advantages of dropshipping is that you do not need to have much capital before you make a sale. You pay the wholesaler only after you got the money from the customer. You also do not have the expense of warehousing the products. Basically, the only thing that you will be responsible for will be serving the customer. If you have an e-bay auction site or even if you have a regular site, customer service is usually minimal. That is if the quality of the dropship items that you sell are good and also if the wholesaler is legitimate. If your supplier will not have the item in stock and a customer has placed an order you will be the one that will have to take care of it. Continue reading to find out the risks involved with dropship items and also how to solve the one major problem regarding dropshipping.

Selling dropship items does entail some risks. If a certain product is not in stock your wholesaler has to let you know because you can not sell an item that the wholesaler will not be able to ship. If a product is backordered or it is not delivered timely to the end customer, you might get a negative rating in e-bay. Negative feedback needs to be avoided of course we all know that.

Being a dropshipper entails the risk of not inspecting the quality of the dropship items being sold. What if the quality is really poor and there are lots of returns?

The fact is that a lot of dropshippers are very successful. The question is what is their secret? They found reputable wholesalers that give them good quality dropship items. How do you know when a seller is honest? We all know that prior to finishing a deal all sellers look honest but once you have placed your order and they are dishonest, the problem is on your shoulders. Finding good wholesalers requires time and effort and trial and error. There is a learning curve involved,in the beginning you place your orders and from good and bad experience you learn which wholesalers are honest and which sellers are just fly by the night kinds of scammers - here today, gone tomorrow.

Imagine there is a way that you can find out beforehand if a supplier is legitimate. Usually the successful dropshippers do not let others know where they buy their dropship items. That is understandable. After all, it is their hard-earned business secret and also they do not want you to sell the same things as they do.

Here comes the good news: There are wholesale dropship directories. These are directories that have lists of wholesale dropshippers that are honest. They check and verify the wholesalers and present to you the legitimate ones. There are thousands reliable, legitimate wholesalers with excellent prices that sell thousands of dropship items.

Knowing these dropship directories before you start selling dropship items online will save you countless hours and tons of money and time. It is definitely a win-win situation.

QUESTIONS YOU MUST ASK YOUR DROPSHIP SUPPLIER

• *What Is Their Order Turnaround?*

When you are selling dropship products, it is usually a good idea to let your customers know that their purchase will be shipped direct from the supplier, so they are aware it may take a little longer to arrive. But you should ask your dropshipping supplier how quickly they turn orders around, so you know how long your customer can expect to wait. It is important you get your supplier to agree to a timescale that works for you, and not the other way round - customers will be put off ordering if they have to wait too long.

- **Which Shipping Service Do They Use?**

How does your dropshipping company ship the items to your customers? Do they use UPS, DHL or another reputable carrier,or do they try to cut costs by shipping your items with a small and unreliable company? Also you need to find out what their standard shipping service is and how long it usually takes to get to the customer. It is of no use having a company that supplies great dropship products at low prices, if your customers have to wait longer to receive them.

- **Do They Provide Tracking Numbers?**

Check whether your dropshipping company provides tracking numbers for their shipments.

Most suppliers will send you a tracking number as soon as the item has left their warehouse. This is for your piece of mind, and so you can give the details to your customer so they can track their delivery - which is just good customer service. Be wary of suppliers who do not offer a tracking number - how will you know if the item has been shipped, or where to find it if it goes missing?

- ### *What Is Their Returns Policy?*

A good supplier will provide quality dropship products for your customers, but even so, there will be times when a customer wants to return an item. May be it is faulty,or they have just changed their mind. Make sure you know what your supplier's policy is on returns; who pays for return shipping, does the customer get a replacement or a refund etc.? This way, you can make sure that your returns policy does not promise anything your supplier will not do.

- ### *What* Fees Do They Charge For Dropshipping?

Some Dropship Suppliers will add fees to the price of the product, to cover the packaging and shipping for the item. Make sure you know all the costs involved in getting the product to your customer, so you can charge a price that still makes you a profit. While some dropshipping suppliers may have a fee for shipping, steer clear of any who try to charge you just to get access to their inventory.

- ### *Are They A Blind Dropshipper?*

A blind dropshipper is one that does not put their company information on the package that goes out to your customer. This is obviously better for your business, as the customer will not be confused when they pay one company and the item arrives from another. Some dropship suppliers will even put your company name on the packaging, which looks even more professional, so it is worth asking.

What Is Their Account Management Setup?

Finally, you want to make sure that after you have placed your order, you know who you can get in touch with to check any details, or sort things out if anything goes wrong. Good suppliers of dropship products will look after their customers, and be keen to develop a long-term, profitable relationship. There is nothing worse than having to chase your supplier for information, when you should be getting on with building your business.

It is important to make sure that, when you have sourced a genuine dropship supplier, you find out how they operate, so you know how to manage your business with your customers. Make sure you ask enough questions to find out if your dropshipping supplier operates the way you had like them to. If they do not, ask them if they can be flexible. If they can not, then despite the fact they seem like a good business, they might not be the right supplier for you.

WAYS BY WHICH DROPSHIPPING CAN HELP YOUR BUSINESS BLOSSOM

Selling goods and services is a highly competitive industry to engage in. One has to exert effort and be quick to adapt to new and better ways to be one step ahead than the others. Business-minded individuals are constantly searching for ways to increase their profit and attract more customers. One technique that businessmen have been using for ages and have been helpful in helping them rake in profits is dropshipping.

If you take time to understand how dropshipping works then you can surely reap profits from the benefits of dropshipping. With the countless possibilities that dropshipping has to offer, many dropship companies have sprouted and are gaining popularity in both online sellers and store owners alike.

In order for one to take advantage of what dropshipping has to offer, it is important to know the four important benefits that dropshipping can bring to help boost your profits.

1. Dropshipping can help you save money spent for inventory purposes without sacrificing the quality of the products that you sell. When you have a partnership with a good dropship company, you can do away with the cost of having to do regular stock inventory since this task is being taken care of by wholesale companies who dropships. It is the responsibility of dropship companies to ensure the quality and inventory of products that you will be selling.

2. Dropshipping helps you to save on money spent for shipping. Wholesale dropshipping companies will be the one to pack and ship all the purchased orders of your customers. Your job is to notify the wholesale supplier of the order and the shipping details. You can use the money you can save on shipping as additional capital for another business venture.

3. Dropshipping companies assure that delivery of the products to your customers is highly efficient and quick. The best dropshipping companies already know the twists and turns of shipping since they have been doing these for many years and have already acquired good feedback. Thus, you should exercise caution when looking and selecting for the best dropshipping company that you can do business with.

What Is E-commerce?

E-Commerce or Electronic Commerce (EC) is the process of conducting business transactions in a virtual economic environment. E-Commerce is becoming a rewarding venture. It is continuing to face challenges throughout the passing years. It has stroke the traditional sales and marketing procedures.

Ecommerce is ideal for niche products. Ecommerce is here to stay, and for many its already second nature when it comes to shopping. Others may need some more convincing that their money and personal details will remain safe should they ever decide to buy something online. Ecommerce is the latest trend in the thriving online business arena. As its name implies, ecommerce is all about electronic commerce and it gives entrepreneurs a completely interactive online platform to make business.

Unemployment is skyrocketing and we are all finding it increasingly difficult to earn a decent living. But there is hope for those of us who need some extra cash this time of year, and that hope is through online dropshipping!

Making money online through drop-shipping is pretty easy if you know what to do and how to do it. One of the best ways to start making money on the Internet is by creating an e-commerce site that will buy and sell various wholesale and closeout merchandise. Making money online through drop-shipping is a wonderful opportunity for many people. But this is fact that some people fail to make money online while others make a fortune with this opportunity.

Dropshipping allows average internet users like you and me to quickly and easily market products online without the hassles of purchasing inventory, packaging or shipping. Simply register with an online dropshipping service, market their products online at your price, and keep the difference after the sale! This service is made possible because dropshipping companies anonymously ship their products directly to your customers. As far as your customer knows, he is dealing exclusively with you and your online business.

eBay and Amazon.com are great options for those new to dropshipping online. With minimal costs, new dropshippers can test the waters of online e-commerce and attempt to resell high demand products to a wide customer audience. Although eBay may charge a nominal listing fee to sell your product, Amazon.com will generally only collect a small percentage when your product actually sells. Or, better yet, market a variety of products from your dropshipping supplier on your own e-commerce website and quickly build a loyal customer base.

The first step to getting started in the world of dropshipping is to find the right supplier. Be extra careful in choosing your supplier because not all dropshipping websites are run by true product wholesalers. One of the biggest dangers in the dropshipping business is finding a supplier who is really a middleman; if you do not find a real supplier, the product pricing will be higher and your profits will be lower! Rather than searching for suppliers through a search engine, I recommend that you sign up for a database to ensure that you have access to the best products at the most affordable prices!

Once you have found your suppliers, the rest is easy! Simply select the products that you wish to resell, post those products in an online auction or on your own e-commerce website at a slight markup price, and wait for customers to purchase your products. When your sales start rolling in, simply forward the order information to your dropshippers and they will handle the rest!

Dropship model is highly required as an option for sourcing products, as an Ecommerce store owner. It is a method of identifying a supplier that will ship products to your customers directly as they are ordered. Another alternative for sourcing products is, to buy a large stock of inventory, store the stock in a warehouse or garage, and then package them manually and ship to your prospective buyers as they ordered them.

Whenever possible, it is suggested that you use the first option to source products for your business even though, the two options have their peculiar set of pros, and cons. However, I believe that the pros of the first option above overshadow the coins based on years of experience. On the other hand, using a dropshipper is better than stocking the inventory yourself.

However, three basic processes are involved in the dropshipping model. The first process is that, the customer will place his order on your website and pay in full for the retail price of the product; you will then send the order information to your supplier, who will charge you a wholesale price that is low. Finally, your supplier ships the product from his factory to your customer directly.

However, there are many reasons why you need this model in question for your Ecommerce store. **The number one reason** is that, you are not required to make any up-front purchase that can cost a lot of money sometimes. With this model we are highlighting, you do not pay a dime to your supplier, until when you collect payment from your customer. This particular arrangement is not only beneficial for cash flow purposes; it equally ensures that you never have obsolete stock items that nobody will buy in your store.

The second reason why you need this model for your business is that, you do not have to waste your hard-earned money on warehouse, or other equipment to handle process orders. All you need for your Ecommerce store is your home computer, and nothing more. Therefore, you will save a lot of money on buying equipment, paying rent, hiring staff to run the warehouse, and all other overhead costs attributable to the business. Consequently, your monthly expenses will drop drastically when you employ the service of a dropshipper.

The third reason is that, you do not have to give yourself sleepless nights over processing, and shipping of orders to your customers. Your dropshipper who is the supplier will take care of that. All you need is, to send all the details relating to the order to the customer, and also forward the shipping tracking information to the customer as soon as you receive it from the supplier as well.

On a final note, using a dropship model for your Ecommerce business will allow you to concentrate all your time, and effort on getting customers to your online store. You will end up spending the whole time you have in this world, if you decide to warehouse and ship products yourself rather than using the limited time you have to increase traffic to your site.

Dropshipping is a marvelous innovation in the eCommerce business. A dropship website lists products online, but the seller does not physically keep stocks on hand. The products are with the wholesale dropshipper. The seller simply markets the products, takes down orders and collects payment. He pays the dropshipper who then ships the item directly to the customer. It is an easy way to make money while working from your own home and there is no need for upfront money to buy stocks in advance. Here is how you can establish your own dropshipping business:

1. Find A Reliable Dropshipper.

A search on the internet will yield hundreds of dropshippers. Many of these are middlemen who may charge participation fees or require a minimum monthly order. Find a dropshipper who will not charge monthly fees. It is even a good idea to look for wholesalers and ask if they are willing to dropship. When you sign up with a dropshipper, you will be required to provide your full name, business name and contact information. Applicants from the United States may be asked for their SS number and tax number for tax purposes. You may also be required to have a credit card on file.

2. Select Items From The Dropshipper's Stocks For You To Sell.

Conduct a market research and choose the items that you think will sell quickly and profitably. Check out the prices of these items on the sites of other sellers so you will know if your prices are competitive and if you can make a decent profit on your markup.

3. Build A Dropship Website Or Set Up An Online Selling Site.

You can sign up for an eBay seller's account or have your own dropship website which the dropshipper may provide for you to use. List the items on your selling site. The dropshipper usually provides stock photos of the items. You can also use the wholesaler's product description. Make sure that the price of the item reflects its cost plus eBay fees and your profit. If you sell on eBay, you will be required to have a PayPal account because eBay will not allow any other form of payment.

4. *Market Your Product To Attract Customers.*

Your job as the seller is to attract customers and increase sales. Use emails to provide free advertising for your dropshipping business. Let your existing customers know of new products or special sales. You can also use banner ads or pay-per-click sites, but remember that this will entail additional costs.

5. Order And Pay For Products Sold To Your Customers.

Every time you make a sale, order the item and pay your dropshipper. Give the drosphipper your buyer's shipping address and the dropshipping company will package and ship the item directly to your customer.

To avoid fake wholesalers and dropshippers, it is a good idea to use a wholesale directory like SaleHoo. It saves you the trouble of having to check if the supplier is legitimate because SaleHoo screens and verifies all suppliers on their database. Find dropshippers and wholesalers on SaleHoo for products that you can dropship for a profit.

The process of dropshipping is not a new concept. Savvy business men and women have used it in the past to sell merchandise through catalogues and teams of salespeople going door to door. With the advent of the internet, however, and personal auction sites like Amazon and eBay, this form of business is now reaching a much wider audience.

What Is Dropshipping And Why Should I Use It?

Dropshipping is a sales technique where you, the seller, list a series of goods a manufacturer provides as items you have for sale. When you make a sale, you then place the order for the product with the manufacturer and keep the difference in cost from your price to the wholesale price. The manufacturer then fulfills the customer's order and ships it to them.

Considering that you are the customer's direct link to a manufacturer, there is less room for error when dropshipping.

Each item is also made to order and shipped directly to the customer from the wholesaler, reducing the risk of product damage from being passed between providers. For these reasons, some customers may be searching specifically for a dropshipper, which expands their relevance in the market and their population in the future.

Why eBay and Amazon?

While drop shipping can be used in many different ways on the internet, sites like Amazon and eBay make the process even easier. Each site allows users to create accounts and upload auctions for their own personal items. What this means for drop shipping is that you have access to a safe, world wide marketplace with an easy-to-use interface and a massive, pre-existing user base.

Amazon and eBay also offer advanced search options that help you find best selling products. This option can help you determine the price, availability and popularity of the products you wish to sell. In some instances a site like these may even offer help in advertising your products.

These sites can also help build your small businesses reputation. Since both use a form of user ratings, where customers rate your performance, a consistently good rating will help your business grow in popularity and increase your profits. While Dropshipping can be used as a means to make money, it can also be used as the beginning to a business that will later expand beyond the internet.

There are other venues that one might use to dropship, but part of the reason eBay and Amazon are as appealing as they are, is the way they combine numerous elements into one cohesive whole. You can purchase items on these sites to own or sell. You can sell your personal items, and manufacturer items with dropshipping. And you are provided with all of the researching tools to find how best to sell and purchase your products. With all of these advantages in individual sites, it provides the perfect gateway into the world of dropshipping.

Tips On Finding The Best Dropship Company And Make Money On ebay And Amazon

This business venture can be seen everywhere on eBay and Amazon, you are just not aware of it. How do you think an eBay seller can list 20,000 items and ship them at the same time? This is pure drop shipping and the biggest sellers are doing it.

The best drop ship company should give you access to thousands of products to promote. This lets you promote anything you want. By doing some research on eBay pulse, you could see what is constantly selling online. Now since your dropshipper is giving products at a discount price, you set your own price and make your commission.

No more rides to the post office. Dropshipping eliminates the process of shipping and handling. You simply make the sales, take your profit and the shipper does the rest. This automated business at its finest. After you are done you redo the same process and continue making money.

eBay and Amazon are not the only ways to gain customers. You could create your own website and have gained more sales. You could also sell to friends and family and have the products deliver right to there door. By having access to you drop shipper is like having a ware house of supplies.

You are you own boss so you set your hours when you want to work. The amount of money you want to make is all up to you. Have a huge amount of items for sale online could bring you lost of money. The more you have listed, the better chances you have making sales and more profits.

EBAY AND DROPSHIPPING

Thousands of people just like you use eBay auctions on a daily basis to sell and buy products on the Internet; now it is your time to start your own dropshipping home- based business and succeed in the eBay auctions 'game'!

There are no special skills required for this dropshipping business, all you need is a computer, Internet access and some basic computer or Internet knowledge.

Dropshipping is when you sell products on the Web, forward the orders to the dropship supplier and, in return, the dropshipper ships the product to your customer (buyer).

You act as the middleman between the dropshipping supplier and your buyer. You can take orders by credit card, PayPal fax or any other method you can think of. You can sell through your own Web Site, Yahoo store, or even through e-mails.

Your profit is generated on the difference between your selling price and the price the dropshipping supplier charges you.

Thanks to dropshipping you can start making money 'instantly' without any investment in inventory, warehousing, shipping, equipment, employees or office space.

Having products drop shipped by suppliers, allows you to concentrate on truly important aspects like advertising, sales and promotion.

Pay attention! There are lots of companies claiming to be 'Drop Shippers'. However, a legitimate drop shipper is a factory-authorized wholesale distributor, or sometimes the actual manufacturer of the product. A legitimate drop shipper should not charge you an 'account setup fee' or ask you to place a 'minimum quantity order'.

Make sure you find legitimate drop shippers who have the product(s) you want to sell, talk with them on the phone or by e-mail and let them know that you are truly serious about doing business with them.

Customer support counts in the dropshipping business, so do not hesitate to contact dropshipping suppliers before you proceed to work with them.

This will help you decide if you really want to do business with a particular drop shipper or not.

To succeed in the dropshipping business you will have to look for hard-to-find products that people desperately need and want to purchase.

The key is to sell products with little or no competition.

Do some research for product's you want to sell that you think will have little or no competition on eBay.

I suggest you research for quality products and legitimate dropship suppliers, monitor the eBay auction listings to see if there's any competition and test the market (e.g. find out if people really want to spend cash on the product you want to sell)

Remember! Dropshipping makes it easy for you to start and run your own home-based businesses on a shoestring budget; and eBay is the 'perfect' medium to expose your product to potential buyers all over the globe!

Dropship Wholesale Directories - *eBay Business!*

Every dropshipper runs into the problem of finding reliable sellers with good, wholesale prices. After all, having good suppliers is the key to being successful in any eBay business. Thankfully, dropship directories can make this process a lot less painful, and they can make your eBay business more profitable.

Dropship directories compile lists of suppliers and wholesale products to make the dropship process easier. By having hundreds of suppliers in one place, it is easy to compare prices to ensure the greatest profit. In addition, with dropship wholesale directories, support forums give dropshippers the ability to communicate with others in the industry, and customer service can produce hand made dropship lists for whatever niche that is being targeted.

Dropship wholesale directories are usually very good for providing access to the suppliers of knock off or no-name branded goods. While some dropshippers are skeptical of selling these products, they are usually more profitable to dropship than the name brand. In fact, many buyers on eBay are looking for less expensive, alternative options to name brand goods. No name brands of clothing, mp3 players, and fitness supplies all sell very well on eBay due to the increase of interest in cheaper options. However, if one's desire is to sell only name brand goods, there are dropship directories that provide access to suppliers of such products.

There are plenty of work at homers who make good incomes dropshipping without using dropship directories. However, most find that when they start using the directories as a resource, they are able to find a greater variety of products at better prices. As a result, dropshippers can spend less time finding items at the best price and more time listing the items or writing better item descriptions. Because directories give the user the ability to compare prices, the user can easily find the best price to ensure the greatest profit. Some even have access to imported goods that are far below their eBay selling prices. These directories can also be excellent learning tools for those who have a new eBay business.

Dropship wholesale directories should not be confused with dropshipping services that list products on eBay for the user. These "services" are usually shams in the fact that they inflate the costs of their "wholesale" products and charge ridiculous amounts of money for their services. Instead, dropship wholesale directories link up dropshippers to the suppliers so that a relationship can be established. Forming relationships with the suppliers can, in the long run, lead to better service, lower prices, and higher dropship profits.

In order to truly maximize profits in one's eBay business it is important to have a large list of suppliers and an even larger supply of products. Thankfully, dropship wholesale directories make access to these resources much easier, and they are a very inexpensive way to increase your dropship profits.

THE PROS AND CONS OF DROPSHIPPING ON EBAY

Dropshipping is an attractive marketing technique, but when you take it to eBay it becomes a real phenomenon. There are tens of thousands of people running dropshipping business as you are reading this book. Some are making very little profit, some are bringing in decent cash and a few of them are generating huge profits. There are a few pros and cons about dropshipping on eBay that you should be aware of before starting your own dropshipping business.

Let us start with the cons sides. First of all, competition is harsh. If you are new at Internet marketing you might have a hard time adapting to the marketing requirements of promoting your new dropshipping venture. Nothing is set in stone here and rules change over night. The dynamics of an online business will keep you on the tips of your toes most of the time as you cannot afford to let your guard down. Another problem that you might run into is scams. If business is thriving you can also expect fraud to be present. Even if you are scammed on eBay, while dropshipping, it is usually for little cash. This is unpleasant but it will not ruin your business - however it might discourage you from further participating on eBay with your dropshipping goods but do not let this put you off.

Now time for the pros sides, and there is a lot to talk about. Dropshipping allows you to turn into a real marketer without ever worrying about product storage, packaging or shipping. They are all taken care of by the supplier. The ease of using dropshipping gives you more time to concentrate on improving your sales techniques and bringing in more customers. If your business runs well, you may consider, like many have before, to dedicate more time to dropshipping and make this your main income source.

Now even more good news: running your dropshipping business requires a minimal financial investment, usually just an admin fee to cover the administration of setting up your account. With the money you would pay for a night out you can start a successful dropshipping business - you do not need to invest in anything, except for the fees you owe the dropshipper. Of course, you only pay the dropshipper when you make a sale, and you usually get to keep about 50% of the retail price or what ever you set as your percentage mark-up.

Dropshipping is an excellent method to test your entrepreneurial skills and see if you can start a successful business online. With such low financial risks, the only thing that you may loose, if the business does not work, is a few hours of research and a lot of hope. However, some careful documentation on the process and a good sense for what the customers want will most likely set you on the right track and turn your online business into the money making machine you always dreamt of.

With dropshipping and any other business, you can only sell what the public will buy. Do not go overboard with obscure products for your first venture, select high volume, everyday products and you too could have your very own dropshipping business.

HOW TO GET REPEAT BUSINESS FROM YOUR DROPSHIP CUSTOMERS

- *Give Them A Reason To Buy More*

Sometimes it can be as simple as giving them a good enough reason to buy more from you. If you offer discounts on multiple purchases of your dropship products, or offer to reduce, or even remove, the cost of shipping for any extra items or a total spend over a certain amount, some of your customers will need no more encouragement than that. They end up paying less per item, and while your margin on each dropship product might be reduced slightly, the increase in sales means your overall profit will be up.

- *Give Them A Reason To Come Back*

As well as getting customers to spend more with each purchase, successful dropshippers will aim to get repeat business from them as well. Your dropship business will grow a lot faster if you can create the need for each customer to come back and buy from you again and again. The basics of achieving this are not too difficult; great products, at great prices, with great service. However, there are other things dropshippers can do to keep their customers coming back. The simplest way would be, the first time a customer buys one of your dropship products, give them a discount voucher off their next purchase, and may be again every few times after that.

Alternatively, you could give them a reason to come back to your site that does not directly involve making another purchase. If you can build a reputation as an expert in your market, by honest reviews of your dropship products, information and guides on your market, and even "how to" videos on your site, customers will come back for the information, and be more likely to make another purchase. They may even recommend your site, for the free information it provides, to their friends who share the same interest - which means more potential customers for your dropship business.

- **Let Them Know About Your Latest And Best Deals**

You need to keep in touch with your customers though, instead of simply hoping they will come back to your site. When you can afford it, invest in e-mail marketing software like AWeber. This lets you send out marketing information automatically and in bulk, to all your dropship customers. Many dropshippers rely heavily on e-mail marketing to keep their customers up to date on their latest offers, newest drop ship products, or add-ons and accessories that will go well with the items they have already bought. As long as you are sensible and do not hound your buyers, they will feel valued, and likely to come and take a look at your offers with a view to buying.

- **Get Your Customers To Do Your Marketing For You**

You can even make more money from your existing customers in a slightly different way, by enlisting their help in attracting new customers. If your dropship business offers a reward, in the form of a discount or maybe even something for free, every time a customer refers someone who makes a purchase, they have an incentive to help with your marketing efforts. As long as you are providing good dropship products at great prices, and offer good customer service, why would they not recommend you, especially with a little reward for them?

- ***Build Better Relationships With Them***

Social Media has really taken off in the last couple of years, and smart dropshippers have realized its potential for getting their customers to spend more, directly and indirectly. Directly, your dropship business will benefit from having a presence on sites like Twitter and Facebook, offering fans and followers exclusive discounts to encourage them to make new purchases. Indirectly, using these sites, and also the communication power of things like a company blog for your dropship business, means you are building a stronger relationship with your customers - which means they are more likely to think of you when they need to make a purchase in the future.

Attracting new customers can be hard for any business. So when your customer has handed over their money for your dropship product, do not see it as the end of the process, see it as the start of a relationship that offers much more potential for your business.

- ***Avoid The Fake Or Poor Quality Dropship Suppliers***

The biggest challenge for any new dropshipping business, is finding genuine and reliable suppliers. There are many sources you can use to find your supplier, some a lot better than others. As a general rule, you should avoid buying the dropship supplier lists people sell for just a few dollars, As the old saying goes, you get what you pay for - if the dropshippers on the list are genuine, they are unlikely to be much good.

If you find your dropship supplier on the internet, or through a drop ship directory, make sure you check them out properly before you hand over any money. Some scammers can be quite convincing, with half-decent websites that look the part. But check out their business registration details with the relevant authority, make sure all their contact details are genuine, and look for reviews of your dropship supplier on the internet. Even better, ask them for customers you can contact for a reference.

- *Avoid Paying Excessive Fees For Access To A Company's Dropship Inventory*

Most genuine dropship suppliers will make money from sourcing good quality products at competitive prices, and then selling them in enough volume to make a decent profit. You should therefore be wary of any supplier who wants to charge you a fee, just to get access to their dropshipping inventory. While charging a fee in itself does not necessarily mean dropshippers should avoid that supplier, an excessively high fee does - and there are enough good, genuine dropshipping suppliers out there who will allow you to sign up for free.

- ***Overpriced Shipping Costs***

A lot of new resellers focus on the price of products from their drop shipping supplier, and do not take into account the full cost of getting the item to the customer.

Some suppliers even pray on this and will charge high and unreasonable shipping costs, which make them more money, and you less profit. Make sure you know the full cost of dropshipping your chosen products, including shipping charges and other fees. Here is a reliable drop ship supplier that give your good shipping prices.

- ***Incredible Discounts***

Beware of dropshippers who offer incredible discounts on popular products. Most of the time these discounts are based on the Recommended Retail Price (RRP), and the supplier may even be overstating this price to make their discounts look even better. It is unlikely you will be able to sell the product for the RRP, as the customer would probably choose to buy it from an established retailer if it was the same price, so base your discount calculations on what you know you can charge.

Also, even if you still find you are getting an incredible discount compared to other dropshipping suppliers, it could be because the business cuts costs on things like delivery and customer service, something which could mean more problems for you in the long run.

There are many pitfalls you will want to avoid when you are starting your new dropship enterprise, and if you use these tips and your common sense, you should be able to steer clear of the scammers. Make sure you check out any new supplier thoroughly; check reviews, get references, and ask plenty of questions - the stupidest question is the one you do not ask, and any genuine supplier will answer all your questions to make sure you are happy. Above all, remember, if it sounds too good to be true, it probably is.

SEARCH ENGINE MARKETING FOR DROPSHIP BUSINESS

Search engine marketing focuses to improve the visibility of online businesses through major search engines.This is done using the following major search engine marketing techniques:

1. contextual advertising

2. search engine optimization

3. paid inclusion

4. paid placement

Search Engine Marketing Tools

Here are the most popular online marketing tools to increase the number of online visitor of your drop ship website.

Web Analytics

Web Analytics forms an important part of Internet marketing. It is not just a nice to have, it is a must have tool for your search engine-marketing tool.

By looking into server logs and web analytics data,you can understand how many visitors are coming to your website and what is the referral. Visitors are coming from different channels such as: contextual advertising at other websites, major search engines, paid online advertisement or through friend's emails. Web analytics can help you understand how to use the right marketing campaign for your website. Analytics can also help you to determine which locations get consistent hits on your drop ship website, thereby making room for geo-targeting.

Brand Awareness For Your Drop Ship Business

It is important to create brand awareness for your online business, so more visitors will remember your website and keep coming back. Establishing product credibility through branding will help new clients choose your product, and not your competitors. You can increase the brand awareness through social media.

Blogging About Your Drop Ship Products

Another popular marketing tool is blogging. As a marketer you can write about the latest information about specific product and provide tips.You can drive the traffic back to your own website adding a linking the website.

To increase the traffic or online visitor of your blog, you need to add 2 or 3 blog post per week. Every blog post must have an interesting topic and optimized for the search engines. By adding the right keywords in your blog post will help increase the search results.

Blogs are followed by many RSS readers. As soon as a new post is uploaded they receive an email at their RSS reader with the feed link point back to your blog. People that like your blog content often bookmark and share the link within their blog community.

If the blog has interesting and update to date topics, blog readers will keep following your blog and tell their friends about your blog. Blogging is one the most powerful viral marketing tool.

Currently, microblogging can be done through Twitter, where you can broadcast every update of your blog post.

Link Building

Link building will help increase the ranking of the search engine results. Higher ranking in the major search engines such Google, Yahoo and MSN will increase the number of visitors to your website.

Link building is done by can getting other online websites linking to your website. Link building involves reciprocal linking, purchasing links, submitting articles to article directories and more. But avoid exchanging links with link farm, because that will hurt the ranking of your website.

Pay Per Click

Search engine marketing has also received a big traffic boost from the pay per click model of advertising. The advertiser in this case, pays a fixed amount for every click on the ad posted at the major search engines. Currently there are three big Pay Per Click providers:

1. Google AdWords

2. Yahoo Advertising

3. MSN AdCenter

Online PRs

Online PR is another major tool of search engine marketing. Publishing online press releases about product launch, company event or sales increase can help drive more traffic to your website, because many journalist of news writer are looking for new stories. If the story is very interesting, it might be published in the big journals. This will give your website a tremendous boost of traffic. A press release will also help build trust of the company website.

Why Is It So Important To Be A Knowledgable Reseller?

More than anything else, a reseller needs to remain knowledgeable about the industry he or she is working in. The reason for this is that the more knowledgeable the reseller possesses, the more organized, adaptable, flexible, and successful the reseller will be. And, of course, this will boost the success potential of the business enormously.

The Terms

- ***Product Feed:***

A file maintaining all the requisite information about a product list associated with an ecommerce site.

Such feeds provide product information to search engines which aid in reseller inexpensively finding customers.

- ***Data Feed:***

This is a process in which user can receive updated from a data source.For resellers, the ability to stay in the loop with their affiliate service and to keep their customers informed becomes possible.

- **XML:**

XML stands for Extensible Markup Language and it is means of encoding documents electronically. Resellers will employ it to exchange data over the internet in a safe and secure manner.

- **RMA:**

RMA stands for Return Material Authorization which is the process of returning goods or services for replacement or repair. Resellers need a RMA system in place so they are not forced to accept losses on defective products.

- **Import Duties:**

These are taxes the recipient of a package from a foreign company will need to pay on the receipt of certain items. Dropshippers need to know how much customers will pay on import duties so they can adjust their pricing and shipping accordingly.This can help the company still remains cost effective for customers.

- ***VAT:***

VAT stands for Value Added Tax and it is a fee charged on all levels of consumption and sale. Mostly used in Europe, a VAT tax can add upwards of 20% to the cost of an order.

- ***Billing Address:***

This is the address associated with the credit card used in the purchase. Proving a billing address to the reseller allows the reseller to charge the credit card. It also aids in preventing the use of stolen credit card.

- ***Shipping Address:***

This is the specific address the customer would like the order shipped to. It may or may not be the same address as the billing address.

- ***Ecommerce Portal:***

This is an online hub where sellers, suppliers, and consumers can interact.For the reseller, such a portal can greatly expand social media marketing potential.

- ***Merchant:***

A merchant is someone that sells a product directly to a customer.Merchants should not be confused with suppliers which are, in essence, wholesalers that provide products for merchants or retailers to sell.

- **CMS:**

A Content Management System allows for the proper maintenance and management of workflow. Dropshippers will find it enormously helpful to maintain organization.

- **DSR:**

Dynamic Source Routing is designed to effectively route wireless mesh networks which aids the dropshipper with computer networking setups.

- **TOS:**

Terms of Service (TOS) refers to the contractual agreement concerning the rules of working with the dropshipping agency. Violating terms of service could lead to the affiliate being dropped from the main company the dropshipper is affiliated with.

FAQ:

Frequently Asked Question(s) from potential customers.Dropshippers need to know the common FAQs associated with their business so they can put them up on a special page on their website.This can eliminate a lot of time responding to the same customer inquiries over and over again.

- ## SKU:

Stock Keeping Units are common identifiers for products.Maintain lists of SKUs can ensure a dropshipper knows exactly what is in an inventory at a particular time.

- ## Listing Software:

This is software designed to presents proper listings of products and merchandise.Dropshippers can use this software to more effective present eBay or other listings.

- *Merchant Account:*

A bank account that allows a company to accept credit and debt card payments. Such an account provides more convenient payment options to the dropshipper from the customer.

- *CAN-SPAM:*

This is a law passed in the United States that places restrictions and regulations on how a seller can promote a direct email campaign.

Dropshippers employing mass emailing marketing strategies need to be in compliance with such regulations or face fines and other penalties.

- *Shopping Cart:*

This is a software program that allows customers to add pending purchases to a section of the website where purchasing can be completed when all the items the person wishes to purchase are "placed" in the cart.Such software is vital to dropshippers since it makes online purchasing more streamlined and less cumbersome.

- *Affiliate:*

An affiliate is an associate of a retail service that sells on a consignment or commission basis. Dropshippers would be the affiliates of the dropshipping service that actually warehouses and ships purchased items.

- *Chargeback:*

This is when a financial institution forces a refund to a customer.In many ways, this keeps dropshippers honest since a third party (a financial institution) can hold them to certain standards. However, it is sometimes used by unscrupulous people to get their products for free.

- ***Email Client:***

Specialized software program designed to manage email accounts.This makes the process of managing email much easier for the dropshipper.

Please take note of them!!!

✓ ***Find A Manufacturer That Sells Products You Believe In***

You are more likely to endorse and sell products that you have a personal interest in.Think of it as your own personal business and try to spread your products to the widest possible audience. Companies like Worldwide Brands offer databases to search for potential wholesalers that fit your agenda.

✓ *Make Sure Your Manufacturer Is Professional*

Though you may want to sell interesting products, it will do you little good if the manufacturer is slow in responding to you. You are their salesman and they should treat you professionally. If they fail to do this, then do not hesitate to change to one that works.

✓ *Amazon and eBay*

While you could create a website for your small business or a special catalogue to send to potential buyers, it is better to start smaller.

Amazon and eBay offer the tools to begin dropshipping quicker and with less hassle.

✓ *Look For Marketing Trends*

Take some time to do research and find what products are selling the best. Even though, as a dropshipper, there is no physical product to gather dust, you want to have items that people wish to buy. Make the most of your Amazon and eBay listings so that a good amount of your transactions are successful.

✓ *Price Difference, Rather Than Price Total*

Since you do not purchase anything until after payment from the buyer is received, there is no limit to the price on items you can sell. However an expensive item does not always equal high profit. What matters is the difference in the wholesale price versus your asking price. Set prices so you can make a profit on all different price ranges.

✓ *Offer What No One Else Is Offering*

Dropshipping allows for a wide range of products to enter the marketplace. One could sell homemade items or small business merchandise that larger retailers do not have access to. When determining which items to sell, do not simply consider popularity, but rarity as well. Unique and rare items can sometimes have higher appeal.

✓ *Be Professional*

When selling any product online you want potential buyers to know that you mean business. Provide the necessary contact information and be prompt in your responses.

You want your customers to feel confident that you are a seller and not a scam.

✓ *Start Small*

On websites like eBay and Amazon, customers judge your credibility on your seller rating.Users who buy your products will give you a score and comments based on how well you did. New sellers will always start with a blank slate, so to build your reputation, sell smaller. Lower priced items will make users feel you are less of a risk. After enough successful transactions, you can build your stock.

✓ *Do Not Be Afraid To Ask For Help*

If this is your first time as a seller for a dropshipper, you may find yourself overwhelmed. Research is your best friend, but you can also gain insight and credibility by joining a wholesale dropshipping club. These clubs can help you access more manufacturers, get better prices, and provide a network with which to ask for advice.

✓ *Research, Research, Research*

If you are not prepared to do the necessary research to find the proper manufacturer, locate top selling products, or join reputable drop shipping clubs, then you might consider a different option. Becoming a successful drop shipper involves knowing the field and navigating it successfully. The proper research can help prevent a lot of missteps along the way.

CONCLUSION

Unarguably, dropshipping is a great investment, considering the fact that most people now make use of the Internet to search for goods. Dropshipping is a proven technique for retailers who want to maximize the vast amount of opportunities in various market places all over the Internet.

Made in the USA
Lexington, KY
22 February 2019